Pepperoni or Sausage?

A Book about Conjunctions

amicus readers 3

by Cari Meister
illustrated by Holli Conger

amicus readers

Say Hello to Amicus Readers.

You'll find our helpful dog, Amicus, chasing a ball—to let you know the reading level of a book.

1 Learn to Read

High frequency words and close photo-text matches introduce familiar topics and provide support for brand new readers.

2 Read Independently

Some repetition is mixed with varied sentence structures and a select amount of new vocabulary words are introduced with text and photo support.

3 Read to Know More

Interesting facts and engaging art and photos give fluent readers fun books both for reading practice and to learn about new topics.

Amicus Readers are published by Amicus
P.O. Box 1329, Mankato, MN 56002
www.amicuspublishing.us

Illustrations by Holli Conger
Editor Wendy Dieker
Designer Heather Dreisbach

Printed in the United States of America.

10 9 8 7 6 5 4 3 2 1

Library of Congress Cataloging-in-Publication Data
Names: Meister, Cari, author. | Conger, Holli, illustrator.
Title: Pepperoni or sausage? : a book about conjunctions / by Cari Meister ; illustrated by Holli Conger.
Description: Mankato, Minnesota : Amicus, [2017] |
Series: Say what? Parts of Speech | Audience: K to Grade 3_
Identifiers: LCCN 2015041494 (print) | LCCN 2015046772 (ebook) | ISBN 9781607539353 (library binding) | ISBN 9781681510590 (eBook)
Subjects: LCSH: English language--Conjunctions--Juvenile literature. | English language--Grammar--Juvenile literature.
Classification: LCC PE1345 .M45 2017 (print) | LCC PE1345 (ebook) | DDC 428.2/4--dc23
LC record available at http://lccn.loc.gov/2015041494

A conjunction is a joining word. It joins words, phrases, and sentences.
The **purple** words in the story are conjunctions.

Arjun, Nora, **and** Ping are making pizza. Yum!

Arjun finds the toppings.

"I have meat **and** vegetables for our pizza," he says. "What toppings do you like, Ping?"

PEPPERONI
Olives
Sausage

Olive
PEPPERONI

"I like pepperoni and black olives," says Ping.

Nora says, "I don't like either pepperoni or olives."

"What do you like, Nora?" asks Arjun.

"I like onions, peppers, and sausage," says Nora.

"I like onions, but not peppers or sausage," says Ping.

"What do you like, Arjun?" asks Ping.

Arjun smiles. "I like anchovies and jalapeños."

PEPPE
Olives

Jalapeños

"What are we going to do if we can't agree?" says Nora.

"We need to figure this out because I am starving!" says Ping.

"I have an idea," says Arjun. "Since we can't agree, we can make three pizzas."

The friends make three small pizzas.
Then they put them in the oven.
The pizzas are ready. Yum!

ICE CREAM
CHOCOLATE
Caramel
COCONU

"Who wants some ice cream?" Arjun asks.

He gets out chocolate sauce, blueberries, caramel, coconut, and strawberries.

"Nora and Ping, what toppings do you like?" he asks.

"Here we go again!" laughs Nora.

Jobs of a Conjunction

Conjunctions connect words in a list.

Arjun, Nora, and Ping are making pizza.

Conjunctions connect phrases.

We need to figure this out because I am starving!

Conjunctions connect ideas.

The friends make three small pizzas. Then they put them in the oven.

Sometimes conjunctions are used in pairs.

I don't like either pepperoni or olives.